# A Child's First Book About Hawaii

## Cassandra Land-Nelligt

PRESS PACIFICA

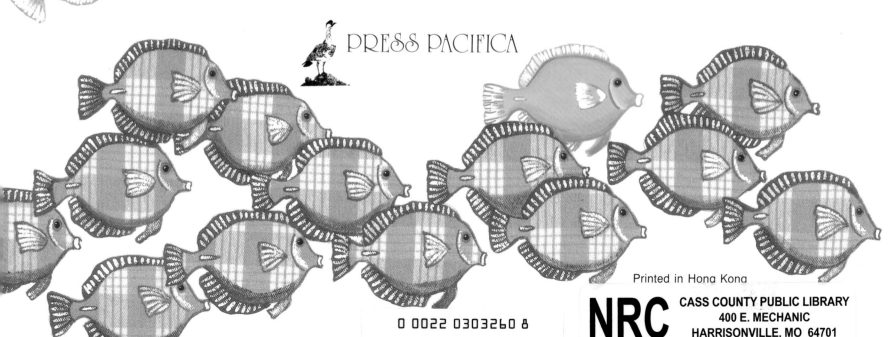

Printed in Hong Kong

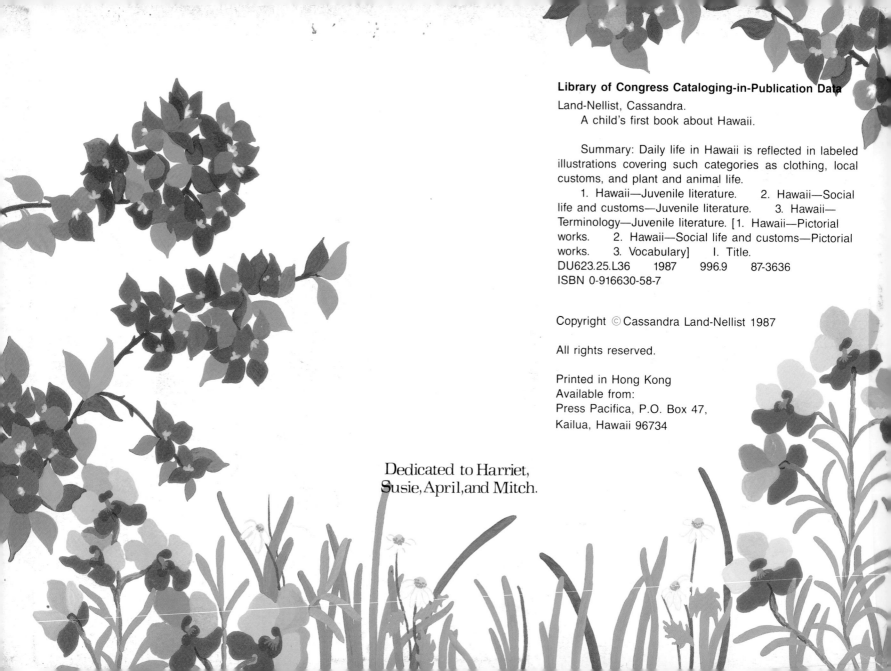

**Library of Congress Cataloging-in-Publication Data**

Land-Nellist, Cassandra.
    A child's first book about Hawaii.

    Summary: Daily life in Hawaii is reflected in labeled illustrations covering such categories as clothing, local customs, and plant and animal life.
    1. Hawaii—Juvenile literature.    2. Hawaii—Social life and customs—Juvenile literature.    3. Hawaii—Terminology—Juvenile literature. [1. Hawaii—Pictorial works.    2. Hawaii—Social life and customs—Pictorial works.    3. Vocabulary]    I. Title.
DU623.25.L36     1987     996.9     87-3636
ISBN 0-916630-58-7

Printed in Hong Kong
Available from:
Press Pacifica, P.O. Box 47,
Kailua, Hawaii 96734

Dedicated to Harriet,
Susie, April, and Mitch.

grandfather
tūtū kāne

brother
kaikua'ana

father
makua kāne

baby
keiki

sister
kaikua'ana

grandmother
tūtū

cat
pōpoki

dog
'īlio

mother
makuahina

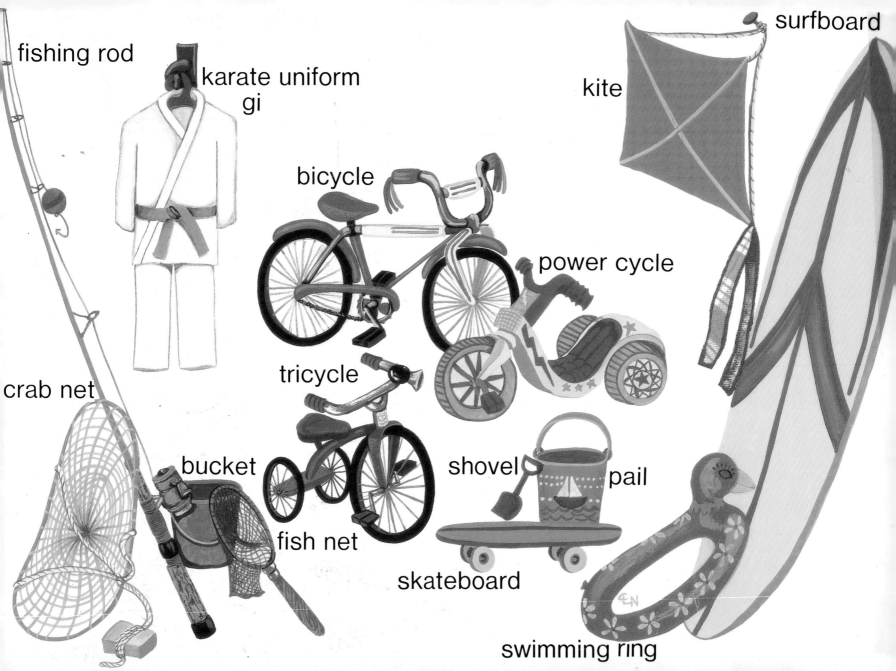

fishing rod

karate uniform
gi

bicycle

surfboard

kite

power cycle

crab net

tricycle

bucket

shovel

pail

fish net

skateboard

swimming ring

wok

pitcher

glasses

plates

pot

frying pan

cup

saucer

fork

mug

record player

rice bowl

spoon

knife

hibachi

MOVING VA

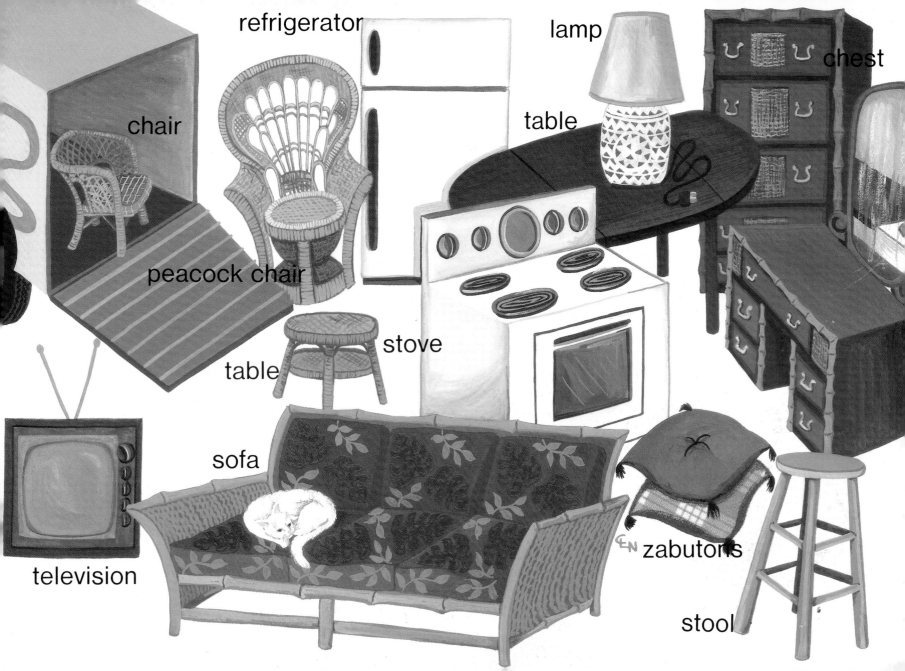

refrigerator

lamp

chest

chair

table

peacock chair

stove

table

sofa

zabutons

stool

television

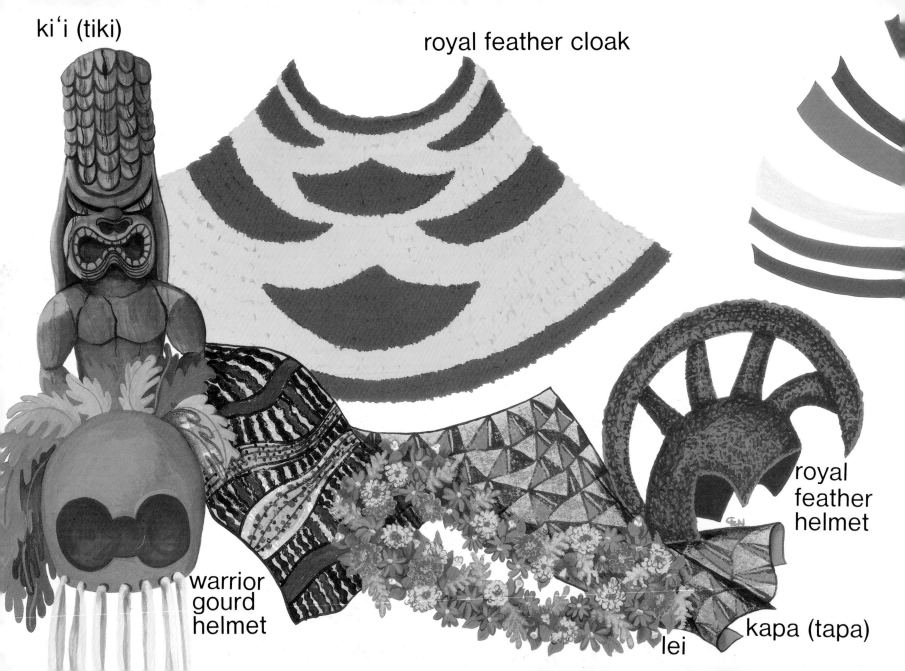

ki'i (tiki)

royal feather cloak

royal feather helmet

warrior gourd helmet

lei

kapa (tapa)

kimono

fire crackers

Boy's Day flying carp

Chinese lion

Girl's Day kokeshi dolls

lucky welcome cat

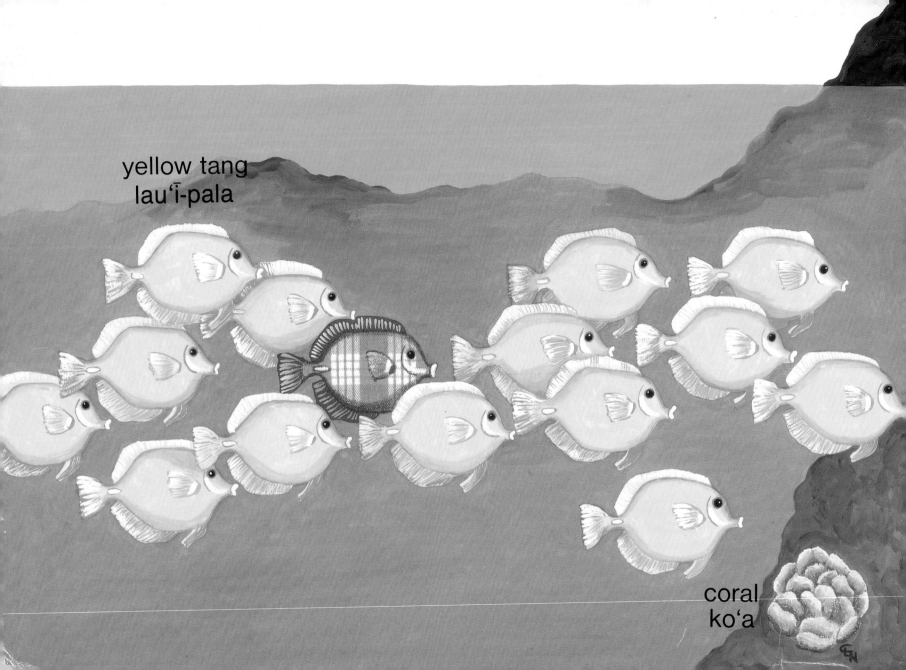

yellow tang
lauʻī-pala

coral
koʻa

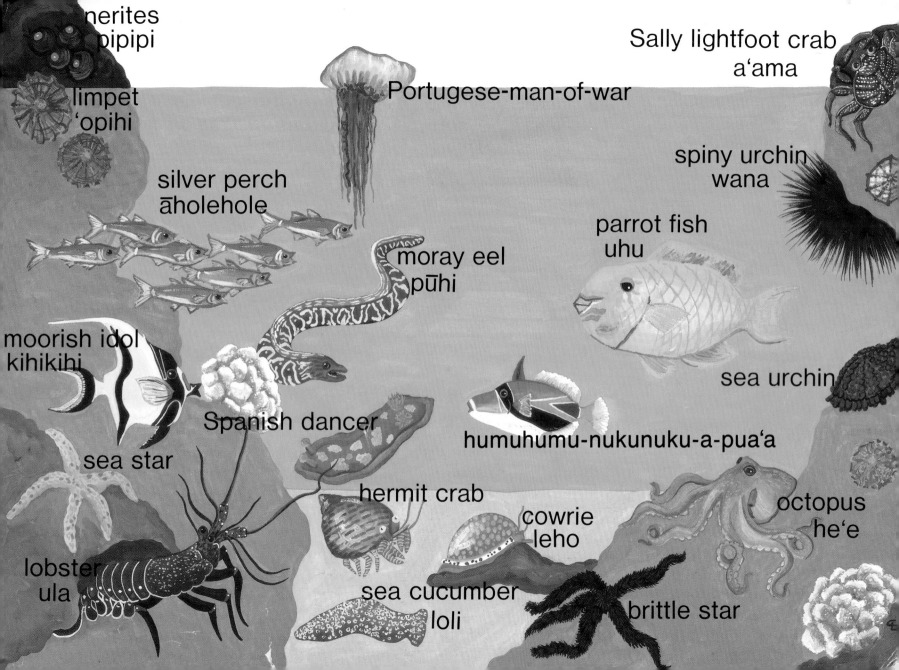

flying fish
mālolo

Hawaiian monk seal
ilio holo i kauaua

spinner dolphin
naiʻa

humpback whale
koholā

Hawaiian
green turtle
honu

jack
uluʻa

manta ray
hāhālua

Pacific blue marlin
aʻu

yellow fin tuna
ʻahi

skipjack tuna
aku

hammer head shark
māno kihikihi

dolphin
mahimahi

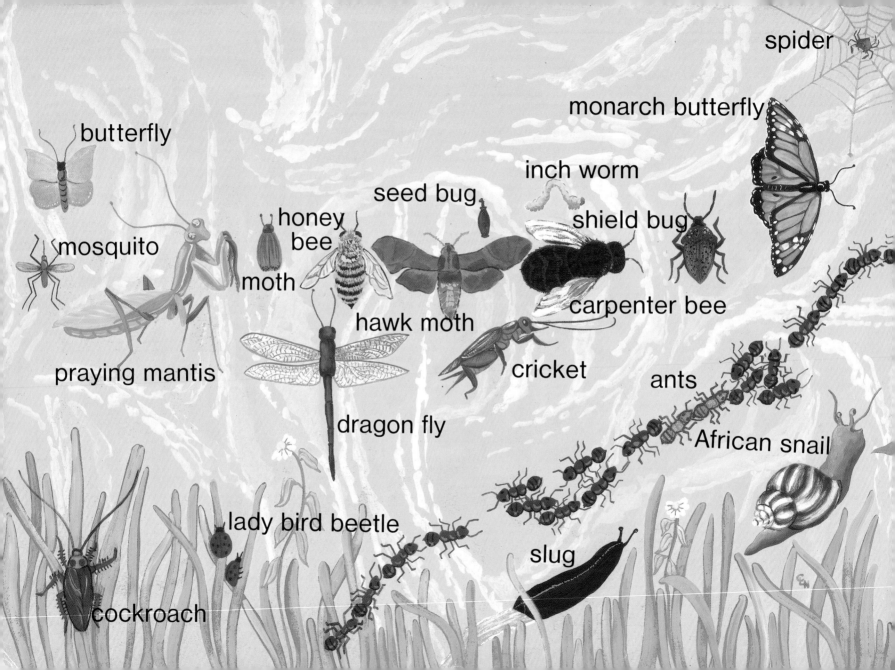

spider

monarch butterfly

butterfly

inch worm

seed bug

shield bug

mosquito

honey bee

moth

hawk moth

carpenter bee

praying mantis

cricket

ants

dragon fly

African snail

lady bird beetle

slug

cockroach

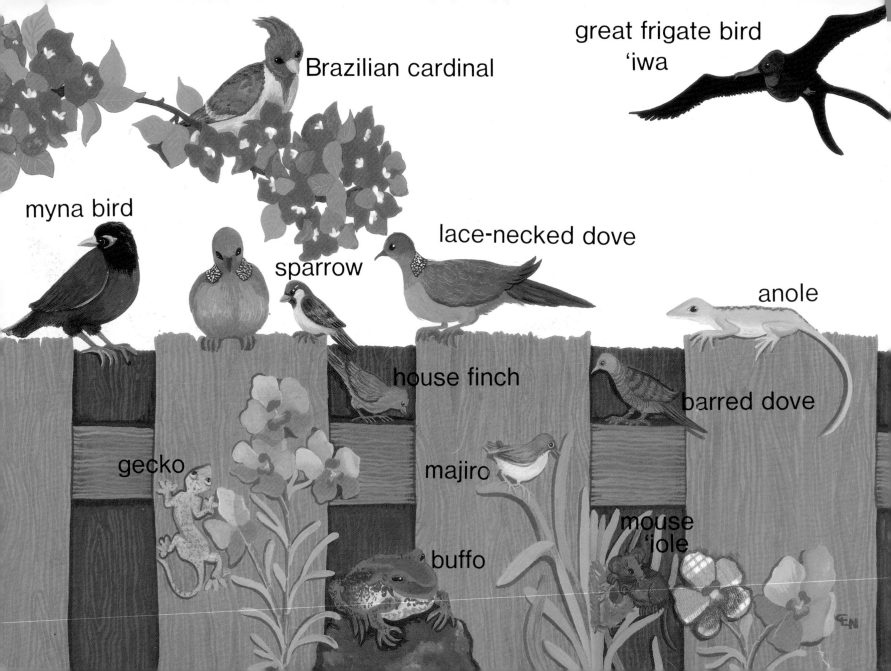

Brazilian cardinal

great frigate bird
'iwa

myna bird

sparrow

lace-necked dove

anole

house finch

barred dove

gecko

majiro

mouse
'iole

buffo

rooster
moa-kāne

longhorned cattle
pipi

horse
lio

goat
kao

mongoose

pig
pua‘a

Hawaiian goose
nēnē

shamisen

ukulele

guitar

drum
pahu

backyard singing

Philippine tinikling dance

hula hālau

ipu

bamboo
rattles
pūʻili

feather
rattles
ʻulīʻulī

Hawaiian chanter

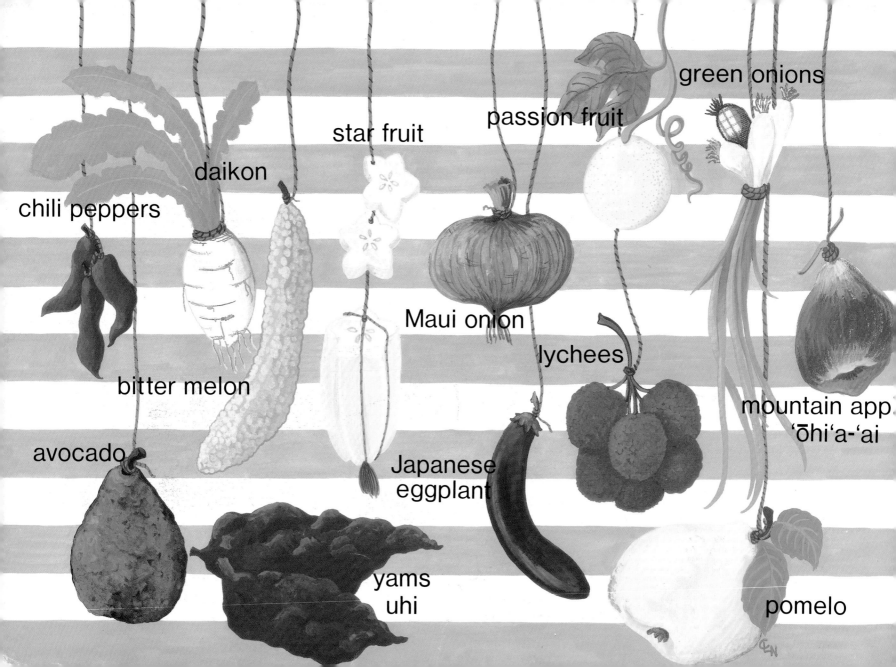

green onions

passion fruit

star fruit

daikon

chili peppers

Maui onion

bitter melon

lychees

avocado

Japanese
eggplant

mountain app.
'ōhi'a-'ai

yams
uhi

pomelo

won ton soup

teriyaki

shave ice

pineapple
hala-kahiki

papaya

manapua

plate lunch

bananas
mai‘a

lumpia

coconut juice

laulau

macadamia
nuts

poi

sashimi

haupia

sugar cane
kō

ginger

sushi

guava

guava juice

garlic

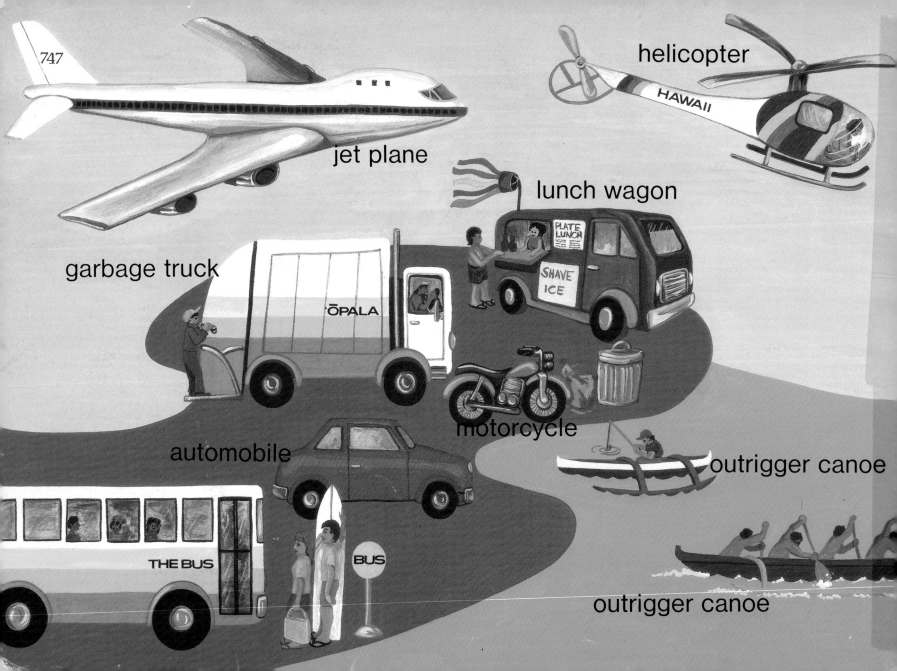

ocean liner

surfer

catamaran

tourist catamaran

double-hull sailing canoe

fishing boat

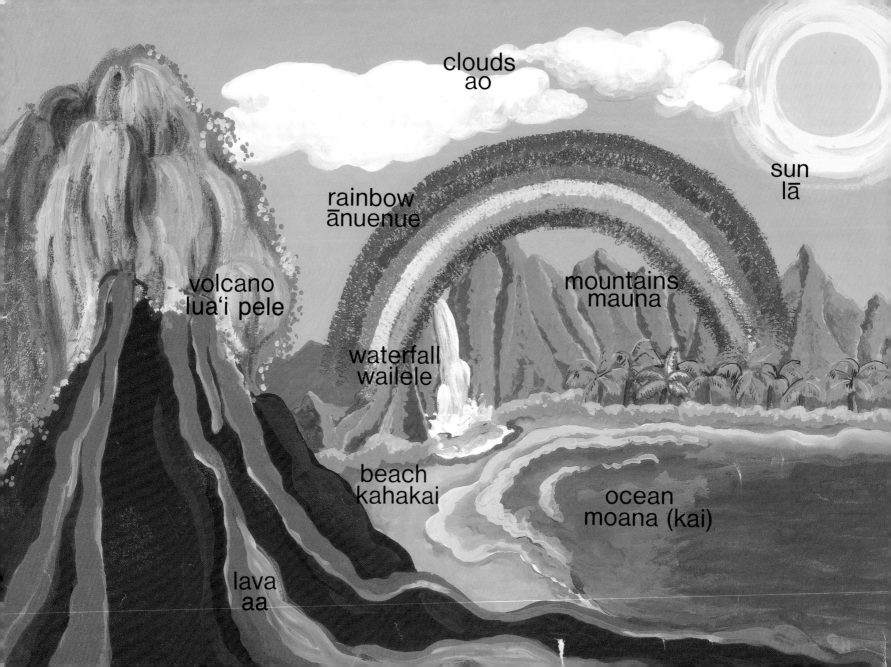

clouds
ao

sun
lā

rainbow
ānuenue

mountains
mauna

volcano
lua'i pele

waterfall
wailele

beach
kahakai

ocean
moana (kai)

lava
aa